BARRON'S

Monika Lange

My Rat
and me

Photographs: Christine Steimer
Illustrations: Renate Holzner

Stories: Gabriele Linke-Grün

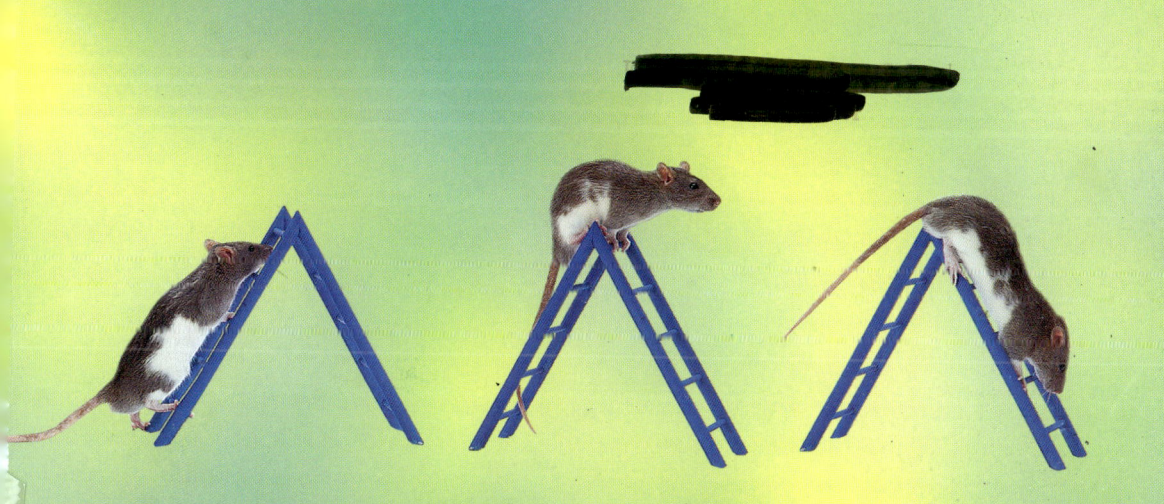

CONTENTS

Contents

Typical Rats
watch it

Descendants of World Travelers 14

Life Underground 14

Rats Defend Their Territory 16

Table: What Rats Are Like 16

Community Living 17

TIP from the BREEDER 18

Many Offspring 18

What Rats Eat 19

A Wary Rat Lives Longer 19

Domesticated Rats 21

The Senses at Work 22

Typical Behaviors 23

TIP from the VETERINARIAN 23

Test: How Well Do You Know Your Rat? 25

Golden Rules for Care
take care

10 Golden Rules for Equipment 7

10 Golden Rules for Feeding 9

10 Golden Rules for Care 11

CONTENTS

Building Trust from the Start

love it

TIP from the THERAPIST	28
A Foundation of Trust	28
Settling In	28
Children and Rats	29
Table: Your Rats' Wish List	29
Fold-out Pages: Building Trust Step by Step	32
Table: Compatibility Test	35
Fold-out Pages: Roaming Free	36

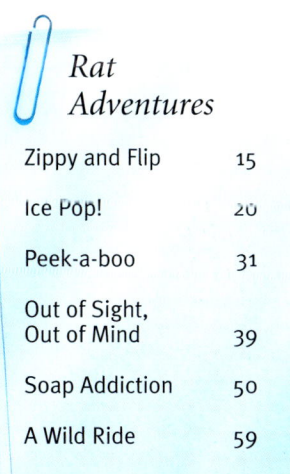

Rat Adventures

Zippy and Flip	15
Ice Pop!	20
Peek-a-boo	31
Out of Sight, Out of Mind	39
Soap Addiction	50
A Wild Ride	59

Fun and Games with Rats

have fun

Fold-out Pages: An Adventure Playground for Rats	42
Build an Adventure Playground	43
Test: What Is Your Rat's Personality Type?	47
Play and Exploration	48
What Your Rats Like	48
Test: How Happy Is Your Rat?	49
Can Rats Learn Tricks?	51
Biting	51
TIP from the PET STORE	51

Active and Happy in Old Age

old & happy

How Long Do Rats Live?	54
How to Recognize an Older Rat	54
Table: The Autumn of Life	54
Age-Related Diseases	55
TIP from the VETERINARIAN	56
How Rats Die	56
Saying Good-bye	57
When a Rat Loses Its Companion	58
Index	60
Addresses	62
Notebook: These Are My Rats	64

TAKE CARE

Golden

Bandita the rat is always ready for a new adventure. Best of all, though, she likes to play with her sister Bandanna. They live together in a spacious cage, enjoy a wide variety of healthy foods, and get along very well with "their" people.

Rules
for Proper Care

TAKE CARE 5

take care

6 TAKE CARE

The 10 Golden Rules for Equipment

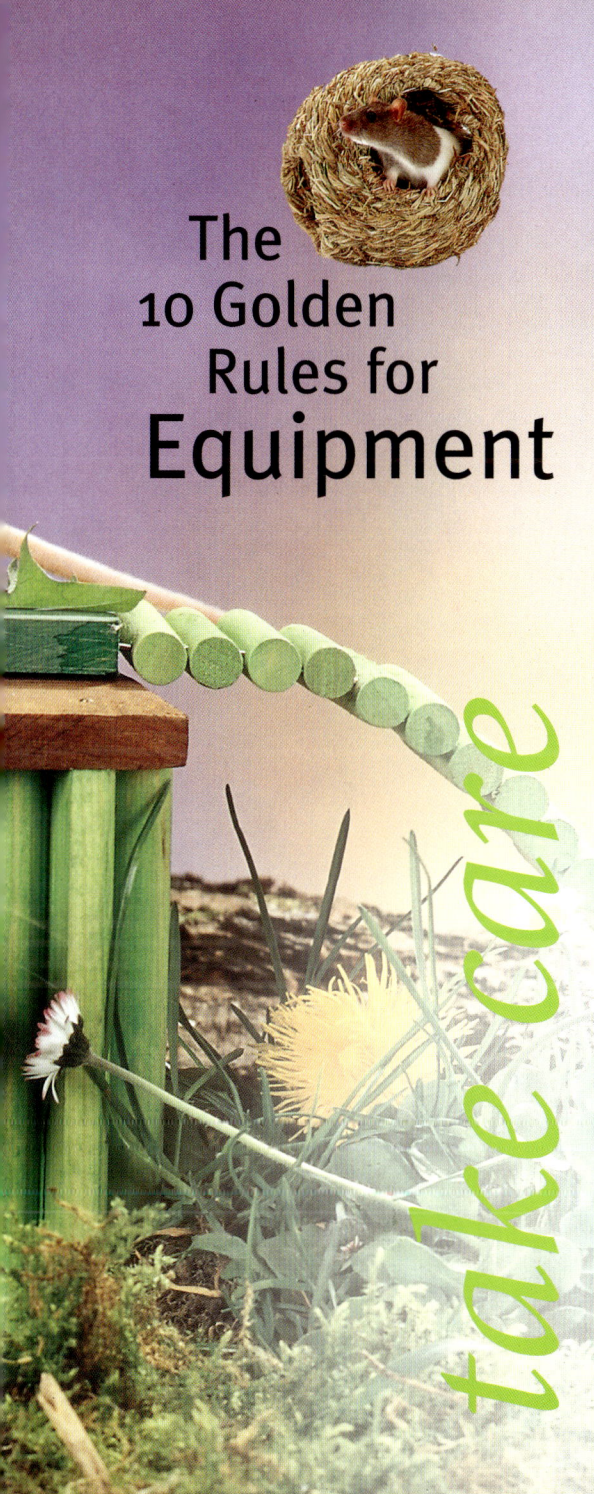

1 A cage for chipmunks or chinchillas, with raised areas reached by ramps or ladders, is the right size for two or three rats.

2 Don't use a wooden cage; the rats would chew right through it, and it would be difficult to keep clean.

3 A floor made of wire mesh can cause sore paws. A plastic pan with high sides will help keep the bedding inside the cage.

4 An aquarium is not a suitable shelter for rats.

5 Choose a heavy feeding dish made of clay or porcelain. An automatic water dispenser is useful.

6 Rats need hiding places inside the cage. Options include the little houses sold for dwarf rabbits, a clay flowerpot turned on its side, or a sturdy cardboard box with a hole cut for a door.

7 Line the cage with a commercial bedding made from paper or plant products.

8 Straw or paper towels make good nesting materials.

9 Place the cage on a solid base in a location that's somewhat elevated and protected from drafts, heat, and cold.

10 Rats need materials to chew on and play with if they are to thrive.

8 TAKE CARE

TAKE CARE

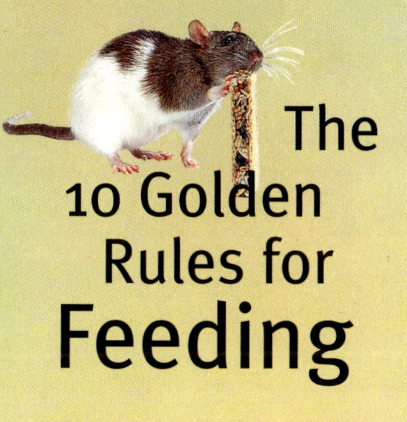

The 10 Golden Rules for Feeding

1 Fresh water must be available at all times. Be sure the drinking tube isn't blocked by an air bubble.

2 For their basic food, offer your rats a grain mixture formulated for rats or hamsters, mixed with sugar-free granola. Store the food in airtight containers.

3 A variety of fresh fruit and vegetables is an essential supplement to the basic diet.

4 Rats are rodents and love to gnaw on hard bread, uncooked pasta and rice.

5 Rats are not vegetarians. Offer small amounts of cooked meat, mealworms, yogurt, cheese, cooked egg, or yeast flakes two or three times a week.

6 Give nuts, cheese, chips, and other high-fat treats only sparingly. Too much fat promotes the development of tumors.

7 Harmful substances include chocolate, caffeine, alcohol, mineral water, spicy foods, raw beans, or vegetables of the cabbage family (including broccoli and cauliflower).

8 Never feed garbage or cheese rinds (they contain a fungicide).

9 Be sure your rats always have some of their basic food available.

10 Rats sometimes eat their own feces (droppings). They need to do this.

take care

10 TAKE CARE

TAKE CARE

The 10 Golden Rules for Care

1 Two or three rats of the same sex are happier than a solitary rat, and they will become just as tame.

2 Once a week, wash the cage and equipment with hot water and replace the shavings and nesting material.

3 Scatter a scoop of the old (clean) shavings on top of the fresh ones so that the cage still smells familiar.

4 Scrub the food bowl and water bottle with hot water once a week.

5 Be sure your rats always have fresh twigs, hard bread, or wood to gnaw on (see small photo, above).

6 If a rat gets very dirty, you can bathe it carefully with cat shampoo. Be sure to dry it well afterwards.

7 Rats need to run free in a rat-proofed room (see page 38) for a while every day.

8 Replace broken toys with new ones, and play with your pet rats every day.

9 Protect your rats against overheating or becoming chilled. Very dry indoor air irritates their respiratory passages.

10 Have the veterinarian show you how to trim claws that have grown too long.

take care

WATCH IT

Typical

Zippy and Flip are lively and inquisitive rats. They've just heard something rustling nearby. Bold Zippy is the first to investigate, while his more cautious brother waits in the background.

Rats

WATCH IT 13

watch it

Descendants of World Travelers

People who keep pet rats must expect to hear remarks that would be considered quite rude if the subject of discussion were a Poodle or a parakeet. Don't let such comments upset you; instead, arm yourself with solid information about your unusual pets.

Our tame rats descend from brown rats that originally lived in Asia. They migrated to Europe along newly established trade routes early in the eighteenth century. At the time, however, it was thought that they spread into Europe from Norway. Therefore, their scientific name is *Rattus norvegicus*. Other names for the brown rat include *Norway rat*, *barn rat*, and *house rat*.

Black rats (*Rattus rattus*), also called *roof rats* or *ship's rats*, are relatives of brown rats, but this species lived in Europe even before the Middle Ages. Black rats originated in tropical Asia and are more petite than brown rats, with bigger ears and a longer tail. In contrast to brown rats, black rats tended to live almost exclusively in the upper stories of buildings, because they are good climbers and prefer warmer temperatures. Like owls, bats, and martens, however, black rats have largely been driven from our lofts and attics.

Life Underground

In the wild, brown rats are highly social creatures. They live together in underground burrows and claim the surrounding area as their territory. The size of the colony and the territory depends on the food supply.

Small colonies consist of about twenty animals; the largest can include several hundred rats. Each colony is established by a few rats, or even by a single pregnant female who digs a nesting chamber in a dry place near a source of food.

Female rats are very good mothers. See how these babies cuddle close to their mama!

Zippy and Flip

My two pet rats definitely have distinct personalities. Flip loves to explore in his own quiet way, but Zippy is a real daredevil. Last night, Zippy had another of his bold adventures. I had been taking care of my friend's two canaries for a couple of days. I deliberately set the birdcage on top of my tallest bookcase, for I could easily imagine that my two rats would be very interested in the visitors. I had been reading comfortably on the couch for a while, with Flip snoozing happily on my lap, when Zippy began to get restless. Finally, he scampered over the arm of the couch and onto the floor. He sniffed here and there, quite innocently, or so it seemed—except for his upright tail, which is always a signal that he is up to something. As I watched, Zippy slowly crept closer to the bookcase. There's no back to the bookshelves, so he was able to crawl in behind them. With his sharp claws digging into the rough woven fabric of the wallpaper and his back pressing hard against the books, he inched his way up the wall. Aha—he was after the canaries! I clapped my hands briskly to deter him, but instead he only climbed faster. As I sprang from the couch to stop him, he slipped and fell. Before I could reach him, however, he had started right back up the wall, undiscouraged by his tumble. The only way to stop my audacious hunter was to pry him from the wallpaper and carry him firmly back to his cage.

Over time, the pack grows and the burrow expands as more nesting chambers, storage rooms, and a network of connecting tunnels and escape routes are added. All the rats maintain the burrow and keep it clean.

The burrow is the central and most important part of the rats' territory. Outside the burrow, wild rats develop a network of beaten paths that lead them to various food sources, provide trails for exploring their territory, and constitute the shortest way to safety when danger threatens. The paths are marked by urine and glandular secretions from the male rats.

Domesticated rats likewise establish certain paths when they roam free outside the cage. If you identify these paths, you can keep them free of hazards, such as electric cords.

Rats Defend Their Territory

Unfortunately, we don't know much about the life of brown rats in their burrows. For one thing, it's difficult to observe the underground behavior of little brown creatures that are active at night. Also, most research has concentrated on eliminating rats as agricultural pests.

What Rats Are Like

→ Rats are rodents and belong to the family Muridae.

→ Rats live in colonies.

→ They are active in twilight and at night.

→ Female rats weigh up to about 10.5 ounces (300 g), males twice as much. Rats measure about 14 inches (37 cm) long, not including the tail.

→ The tail serves to control body temperature, for balance, as a climbing aid, and as a mood indicator.

→ A rat's teeth continue to grow.

→ Rats can grasp food skillfully in their front paws.

→ Domesticated rats live for about two to three years. In their natural surroundings, few rats survive for more than six months to a year.

→ Wild rats become sexually mature at three months of age, and their litters contain six to eight young. Domesticated rats are sexually mature at six weeks and give birth to litters of ten or more.

We do know that rats are highly territorial; males will defend their territory against other rats. In most cases, the intruders quickly retreat when threatened. They instinctively avoid serious scuffles, for even the smallest wounds bring the risk of infection. When an encounter does lead to conflict, the pattern is predictable. First, each rat attempts to intimidate its opponent by arching its back and bristling its fur. If neither rat retreats, the two combatants engage in a boxing match, striking at each other with the strong claws of their hind legs and biting at exposed flanks. The battle is typically interspersed with threatening gestures and urination. If one of the rats surrenders, it will flee or throw itself down flat on its back to placate the victor.

We do not know quite as much about the ranking system of males, but it appears that the biggest and oldest males almost always hold the dominant positions. It's not clear to what extent the dominant rats have priority for food or mating. In any case, it seems to be the younger, lower-ranking rats who must move out when a colony grows to be too large for its food supply.

Community Living

In an established colony, aggression is rare. The rats use a variety of signals to regulate their communal life, and they develop cohesion through interactions such as grooming each other's fur.

Rats love to climb, but these two youngsters haven't quite mastered the ladder.

TIP from the BREEDER

It's quite easy to determine whether a rat is male or female. By the time a male rat is five weeks old, its testicles are clearly identifiable. Likewise, even a lay person can recognize a female by her six pairs of teats: three pairs on her chest and three on her underbelly.

Life in a colony offers a number of advantages. The rats work together to develop a burrow, establish a territory, and find food. Mates are readily available. The branching burrow provides safety from predators. The stored food supply is more or less available to all. It's quite likely that each rat can identify every other rat in the colony by its distinctive odor.

Many Offspring

Brown rats are sexually mature at about three months of age (domesticated rats, as early as six weeks). From then on, in theory, female rats could have a litter every three weeks, because they can mate again immediately after giving birth. They are in heat every three to five days. In the wild, female rats mate with several males within the colony, and the males do not fight over the females. Naturally, this high reproduction rate is important for rats, because the death rate for rats in the wild is also very high.

However, rats don't just produce large numbers of offspring; the females are also good mothers. The gestation period is approximately three weeks. At the end of this time, the female builds a well-padded nest that she defends fiercely against intruders. Sitting on her haunches, she uses her forepaws to help her babies emerge into the world. The mother then eats the placenta, the umbilical cord, and the afterbirth. The newborn rats, six to eight in number, are hairless, deaf, and blind.

In addition to milk and warmth, the baby rats receive regular stomach massages. Otherwise, they would die of constipation. The mother removes their feces and the soiled nest material from the nest. She even works to control the temperature. If she feels a draft, she plugs the hole with clay and grass.

After fourteen days, the baby rats open their eyes. Already eager for adventure, they scramble from the nest. Their high-pitched squeals alert the mother, who fetches them back into the warm nest. (She won't move them from one nest to another, the way a cat moves her kittens.)

By watching their mother, the young rats learn which foods are edible. In fact, they can even taste in the mother's milk what she has been eating. Later, they will prefer these foods if they're available.

By the way, if you don't want your rats to have babies, the safest method is to keep the males and females separated. If you choose to keep a male and a female together, have the veterinarian castrate the male. Be warned, however, that a castrated male remains fertile for as long as six weeks.

What Rats Eat

Rats are omnivorous. They eat grains, fruit, and vegetables; they enjoy cheese, pizza, noodles, and other human foods; they like eggs and milk; and they hunt for insects, snails, mice, and birds. Like raccoons, they fish for insects and minnows along the shore; they plunder fish-traps and dig clams on the beach. Their most plentiful food supplies often arise from human activity. Trash cans and garbage dumps, farmyards, pantries, cellars, sewers, zoos, restaurants, poultry farms—all set an abundant table. The behavior of brown rats gathering food is quite similar to that of bees in a beehive. The returning rats are inspected by the others at the entrance to the burrow. The food they bring and the odors they carry betray whether they have found something interesting. The others then follow the marked path to the food source. Although rats do not hoard food to the extent that hamsters, for instance, do, they do stock reserves of food in special storage chambers. The colony shares the stored food; rats that are not able to forage beyond the burrow can find something there to tide them over.

A Wary Rat Lives Longer

Rats might be said to specialize in non-specialization. They give every new food source a chance, but they do so with extreme caution. The reason may be simply that rats are unable to regurgitate food that doesn't agree with

Body contact is important not only for a mother rat and her babies, but also among adult rats.

Ice Pop!

It was a hot summer afternoon. Zippy and Flip lay idly in their hammock, which I had fashioned from a discarded hand towel and suspended from the bars of their cage. Thinking that they might need a bit of cool refreshment, I went to the kitchen and looked in the freezer for one of their favorite homemade treats. I make these by filling an ice tray with fruit juice, then tucking a fresh strawberry or another bit of fruit in each cube. Once it freezes, Zippy and Flip can lick the ice away and enjoy the morsel of fruit at the end. Sure enough, a supply was on hand, so I brought a fruit ice for each of my little pets. They seized them eagerly and started right in, as the hammock rocked gently to and fro.

Suddenly, Zippy's ice cube slipped from his grasp and rolled under his body. Wow! Was that cold! He leaped from the hammock as if he'd been stung by a bee. Of course, that set the hammock swinging wildly, and Flip tumbled to the ground as well. The ice cubes sailed through the air behind them and landed on Zippy's back. Unprepared for such a volley, my furry friends fled from their cage in alarm.

I'm happy to say that this episode did nothing to dampen their enthusiasm for fruit ices. Now, however, they carry the slippery treats into their little house, where they can enjoy them in peace and quiet.

them, but their caution may also be a behavior developed over many generations of coexistence with humans.

In any case, rats are typically suspicious of changes in their environment. They give any new object a wide berth at first, approaching to inspect it only after several days have passed. If it looks edible, they'll taste it, but they won't eat more until they are sure the food agrees with them. Their marked path then leads other rats to the food source. By the way, not even sewer rats will eat spoiled food. Brown rats will remove from the burrow any stored food that goes bad.

Domesticated Rats

All pet rats are descendants of laboratory rats. Since about 1850, scientists have bred rats for use in research. These laboratory rats have evolved to be quite different from their wild relatives. They are less timid than wild rats and are also less aggressive toward humans. They reach sexual maturity at only six weeks of age, and they give birth to almost twice as many offspring in each litter. Also, the relative size of their organs has changed. Only their social behavior remains largely the same. In fact, if released into the wild under favorable conditions, they can establish colonies that are quite normal.

Basically, wild rats and domesticated rats have the same relationship as wolves and dogs. If only someone had thought to invent a new name for them, perhaps pet rats wouldn't have such an image problem!

As rats have become more and more popular pets, the variety of available color markings has expanded. In addition to the familiar white rats,

Pet rats need constant stimulation and activity. If they are bored, they will not thrive.

commercial ratteries breed pearl, fawn, blue, Agouti, Dalmatian, and many other interesting and attractive strains.

Domesticated rats have not lost their natural curiosity and inventiveness, and like their wild forebears, each rat has its own distinct personality. Because they are such social creatures, they also form close attachments to the humans who care for them.

Rats need to groom themselves daily. With their deft forepaws, they help each other keep their coats clean and healthy.

The Senses at Work

Vision: A rat's eyes specialize in detecting motion, even at a great distance. On the other hand, rats are barely able to focus on objects that are not moving, and they are nearsighted. Because a rat's eyes are located on the sides of the head, it can see what is happening all around it. But the fields of vision do not overlap, so they don't see their environment three-dimensionally. Therefore, rats rely much more on their other senses.

➔ For happy rats: When your rats are roaming freely about the room, be sure to move with extra caution. Because a rat has little depth perception, one of them might unexpectedly run in front of you. You wouldn't want to step on your pet, or even kick it accidentally.

Smell: Odors play a crucial part in a rat's recognition of fellow pack members and also of humans. Rats depend on their sense of smell to detect food. They deposit scent markings on their territory and their paths, and males identify receptive females by odor as well.

→ For happy rats: When you handle your rats, your hands should not carry the odors of perfumed soap, lotions, or household cleaning agents. These prevent your pets from recognizing you by your distinctive personal odor.

Taste: Rats have a fine sense of taste. They react sensitively to anything bitter. Many rats have a sweet tooth, and others are fond of garlic.

→ For happy rats: Be sure to offer your pets a varied diet of healthy foods.

Hearing: Rats can hear ultrasound frequencies. Much of their perception and communication occurs in this range. They squeak in tones that are audible to humans when they signal fear and pain.

→ For happy rats: Rats are crepuscular creatures, most active in the twilight hours. During the day, they need peace and quiet. Keep this in mind when you decide where to put their cage.

Touch: The sense of touch is important for rats. They use their long whiskers to gather information about their immediate environment and to orient themselves in the dark. Rats need physical contact with other rats, as well as mutual grooming, if they are to thrive.

→ For happy rats: Most rats form a close attachment to the humans who care for them;

TIP from the VETERINARIAN

Wild rats live in underground burrows that offer protection from predators. Your pet rats see their cage as the same safe haven, rather than as a prison. Of course, they must have plenty of opportunities to roam free.

your furry friends will respond with obvious pleasure to stroking and cuddling.

Typical Behaviors

Nose in the air: Rats often pause to investigate the odors in their environment. They may stand on their hind legs or lift one forepaw in a posture of alert attention.

Inspecting something new: Rats approach unfamiliar objects warily, with the body stretched forward and always poised for flight.

Marking: Rats mark their territory, and also their human caregivers, with very fine droplets of urine (some rats, unfortunately, with a more copious spray). Males also mark with a glandular secretion.

Nest building: Practically every rat instinctively builds a sleeping nest, using a variety of materials limited only by what happens to be available.

Digging: Rats take advantage of every opportunity to act on their strong instinct to dig a burrow. You'll need to take precautions to protect your houseplants.

Rat yoga: Rats curl up to sleep in positions that might look incredibly uncomfortable. Sleeping for unusually long periods is a sign of neglect or illness.

Grooming: Rats groom themselves several times a day, each time following the same sequence. They also groom each other, thus reinforcing the bonds between pack members. Rough grooming, in which the other rat is pushed down, is an expression of dominance.

Tail: An excited rat will hold its tail erect, stiff as a pencil. A tail held loosely erect signals a more relaxed and adventuresome mood.

Hiding: Dark hiding places give rats a sense of safety and security. When a rat creeps inside your clothing, it finds both shelter and physical contact.

Grinding the teeth: Your rat may rub its teeth together gently to express pleasure as you stroke it. However, grinding the teeth can be a warning signal if the rat also bristles its fur and arches its back.

Hunting: You will observe a rat's hunting instincts when you feed it live mealworms or when it spies a bird or other small animal.

Greeting: When two rats meet, they sniff each other thoroughly.

Estrus: When a female is in estrus (heat), she will respond to a touch on her flanks by flattening her back and twitching her ears rapidly.

Scuffles: Occasional scuffles (in which neither rat is injured) and displays of power confirm the hierarchy of dominance within the pack.

These two rats don't know each other yet. They might get into a little scuffle. If they do, the rat defending its territory will usually force the intruder to run and hide.

How Well Do You Know Your Rat?

The first step to taking good care of your rat is to learn about its behavior and its needs. Here's a little quiz to see how much you already know about your nimble little housemates. The answers are given below—but no peeking!

	YES	NO
1 Are rats solitary creatures?	○	○
2 Do rats have particularly good vision?	○	○
3 Do rats live for more than two or three years?	○	○
4 Does a rat's tail help to control its body temperature?	○	○
5 Do a rat's teeth continue to grow?	○	○
6 Are male rats smaller than female rats?	○	○
7 Are rats inquisitive?	○	○
8 Can rats reproduce when they are just six weeks old?	○	○
9 Will a mother rat fetch her offspring home if they wander too far from the nest?	○	○
10 Do rats that live in the wild have rooms in their burrows that are set aside for baby rats, for sleeping, or for food storage?	○	○
11 Can humans hear all the vocal sounds that rats make?	○	○
12 Will a rat eat food that has spoiled?	○	○

Answers: 1 = no; 2 = no; 3 = no; 4 = yes; 5 = yes; 6 = no; 7 = yes; 8 = yes; 9 = yes; 10 = yes; 11 = no; 12 = no.

LOVE IT

Building

It's a sign of great trust for pet rats to be so relaxed and comfortable in the presence of a human. To develop a good relationship with the rats in your care, you must be sure to respect and meet their needs.

Trust
from the Start

LOVE IT 27

love it

TIP from the THERAPIST

When you bring your rats home from the pet store or breeder, bring along a scoop of bedding from their former cage and scatter it in their new one. The familiar odor will help them adjust to their new environment.

A Foundation of Trust

What do you picture as the ideal relationship between you and your rats? You would like to pet them, play with them, even enjoy just sitting with a warm furry creature asleep on your lap. The rats, in turn, welcome you as a member of the pack—as "family." The little rodents place a great deal of trust in humans. A tame rat will let you examine its teeth, for example, or turn it on its back. Even in an unpleasant situation, a tame rat will usually refrain from biting you.

As with all animals, of course, you must first earn this trust. Rats remember bad experiences, so it's important to start on the right foot from the very beginning. Take care not to provoke the rat into biting—a rat's bite is quite painful, and the incident will damage the relationship on both sides. If it causes you to neglect your pet, the rat in turn becomes less trusting, and so on. In the end, the animal always suffers most; a rat that's left to sit alone in its cage can do nothing to remedy its plight.

Fortunately, all that is needed to build a good relationship is a little sympathetic understanding of the needs of your new pets. If you take the first steps in the right direction, the rest will take care of itself.

Settling In

As you bring your rats home for the first time, imagine what they are experiencing. They have been snatched from their familiar environment and shut up in a box. The pack, their source of security, is gone. In the new cage, they feel helpless and exposed. Might other rats, possibly unfriendly ones, live here? A universe of strange odors besieges them. Every sound is new and threatening.

You can help your new companions settle in by planning ahead, taking into consideration their instinctive wariness. First, be sure their cage and all its fittings are ready, and place it in the location where it will stay. Put your rats in their new home right away, then leave them in peace and quiet. Don't let the whole family and assorted neighbors gather around the cage to inspect the new arrivals. Only the ones who will have the most interaction with the rats should observe them as they settle in.

Depending on the rats' temperament, they will either thoroughly explore the cage right away or hide in the first dark corner they come upon. Watch to see whether they find their food and water and creep into their shelter. Let them have a little nap before you do anything else with them. Under no circumstances should you take them from their new cage before they are ready.

Allow your rats to set the pace for the remainder of the adjustment period. If your new pets have been accustomed to humans from an early age, they won't need to be tamed in the true sense of the word, because they will have no fear of humans. However, they will need to get to know you, your family, and their new environment. See pages 32 to 34 for ways to help them adjust quickly and smoothly.

Children and Rats

Many children like rats. They see them as cute, cuddly creatures, splendid playmates, and affectionate companions. If you, as a parent, help your children learn the right way to treat rats, everyone should get along just fine. Teach

Your Rats' Wish List

What rats like:

1. Shelter and material to build themselves a nest.
2. A clean cage. The ammonia that forms in soiled bedding irritates their respiratory passages.
3. When they greet you, they will want to sniff at your hand.
4. Rats like to be stroked and cuddled— when they're in the mood.
5. Rats enjoy interacting with a playmate.
6. Opportunities for exploration and adventure are essential.
7. Rats like to lie on top of each other, or on top of you.

What rats don't like:

1. Solitude. A rat needs the company of other rats.
2. Boredom. These intelligent creatures thrive on constant activity.
3. Drafts and cold, but also extreme heat.
4. Noise. Rats are especially sensitive to noise in a new environment.
5. Rats detest being picked up by the tail.
6. A sleeping rat will be annoyed if you wake it up.
7. Rats panic when grabbed from above without warning.

your children these important facts about their furry friends:

→ Rats have sharp teeth that they use in self-defense if someone hurts them.
→ Rats are small animals with fragile bones and must be handled gently.
→ Rats like to scurry inside a person's clothing; this can frighten a child who's not expecting it.
→ Many rats will assume that anything inserted between the bars of their cage—including a finger—is food.

Take the rat on your hand and show your child that the rat likes best to be stroked on its head and back. Explain that rats recognize people by their odors, and therefore they like to sniff at fingers. If your children are older, you can show them how to carry their pet in the crook of one arm. It's better for younger children to carry a rat around in a little basket, for example. In any case, you must be sure that the children don't pick a rat up by its tail, which might break.

Rats need regular care. Children should not have sole responsibility for feeding rats and cleaning the cage until they are old enough to carry out the duties reliably. By the way, rats are good pets for teenagers with busy schedules, because the animals are active at twilight and at night. They won't miss the teenagers during the day, and they'll be ready to play in the evening hours.

What fun to scramble around the cat grass—maybe even dig it up!

Peek-a-boo

Flip and Zippy think it's great fun to play peek-a-boo with me. We start with a little wrestling match, with my hand, palm up on the sofa, serving as the mat. Zippy is usually the first to approach. Grabbing my fingers, he challenges me to "wrestle" with him. Then he pretends to be scared, scampering away and hiding under the sofa cushions. Right away, though, he's peeking out again, ready for more fun. Over and over, we play the same little game, sometimes with Flip joining in on Zippy's side, until the two little fellows are tuckered out.

One day last week, we were deep in a vigorous game of peek-a-boo. Zippy and Flip attacked my hand in tandem, then disappeared in a flash behind the sofa cushion. But what was that? The sofa cushion had slipped down into the crevice next to the arm of the sofa, and Flip and Zippy were suddenly stuck. Their heads and bodies had disappeared under the cushion, but their little haunches and tails still protruded. It was a sight to behold! With some difficulty, Zippy and Flip finally extricated themselves and turned around. Cautiously lifting their little heads, they looked at me as if to ask how I could have allowed such an embarrassing incident. Then they stalked off together. The game was obviously over for that day.

Building Trust Step by Step

Have you ever observed people who get along very well with animals? Most of them follow a few simple rules. When they approach an animal, they make their presence known. Hardly any animal likes to be taken by surprise. It's a good idea to say hello to your pet as you draw near. If you call it by name, it may learn to recognize its name.

Animals also appreciate folks who move slowly and calmly. Someone who reaches out suddenly, or tells a story with animated gestures of the hands and arms, appears threatening to an animal who isn't yet tame. Give your rats time to get to know you. If they approach you on their own, that's a good sign. Like dogs, cats, and rabbits, rats recognize others by their distinctive combination of odors. Therefore, part of a polite greeting ritual always involves your pet rat sniffing at your hand.

It's easy to see that these two have become real pals.

1 The First Approach
A rat's day follows a certain pattern of sleeping and waking. Make your first approach when your rats are awake and active, and don't disturb them while they're eating. At first, just watch them, talking to them in a soft and soothing tone. Call them by name. Unless a rat is very shy, you shouldn't try to entice it from its sleeping shelter with a bit of cheese or other tempting morsel.

2 Learning to Recognize Odors
It's important for your rats to learn to identify you by smell. Let your pets sniff at your hand through the cage door. If the rats react with alarm when you approach the cage and disappear into their shelter right away, it's best not to rush them into getting to know you. On the other hand, if they respond with friendly curiosity, you can proceed to the next step.

3 Feeding from Your Hand
Bribery is an acceptable way of making friends. Open the cage door and offer a piece of fruit or other tasty tidbit. You can use a spoon or hold the lure in your fingers. If you offer it on your open palm, a brave rat might even crawl onto your hand. Be sure to give only a little bit at a time, so that your new acquaintances will keep coming back for more!

Roaming Free

A daily period of activity outside the cage keeps your rats fit, both physically and mentally. However, you shouldn't let a rat run free until it is tame to your touch. Otherwise, you'll have a hard time getting your pet back into its cage.

Because rats are cautious creatures, they will explore the room in ever widening circles. Don't give them much food while they roam free or they will have no reason to return to the cage. However, you can take advantage of their instincts in this regard. Wild rats prefer to carry their prey back to the burrow to devour it in safety. If you give your pets a small treat when their time to ramble is over, they will whisk it back to their shelter and you can close the cage door behind them without resistance or argument.

When a rat has free run of the room, everything is an adventure.

Help Your Rats Get Along

The delicate task of introducing two rats to each other will go more smoothly if you follow these helpful hints.

→ Start the new rat in a separate cage, near the first one but out of range for any biting.

→ Let the newcomer get used to you.

→ Switch cages, placing each rat in the other cage for a while, so that they become familiar with each other's odors.

→ Introduce the two rats to each other in neutral territory (the bathtub makes a good spot).

→ Now place both rats in a new (or clean-as-new) cage.

→ Scuffles are normal at first; they serve to establish the ranking order. If the fighting persists, separate the rats and give them more time to get acquainted. If either rat is injured, separate them again and carefully start all over.

Compatibility Test

	Rat	Hamster	Rabbit	Guinea Pig	Dog	Cat	Bird	Mice
Rat	🙂❤️	💣	💣	💣	🙂	💣	💣	💣
Hamster	💣	💣	💣	💣	💣	💣	〰️	💣
Rabbit	💣	💣	❤️	🙂	🙂	🙂	〰️	💣
Guinea Pig	💣	💣	🙂	❤️	💣	💣	〰️	💣
Dog	🙂	🙂	🙂	🙂	🙂❤️	🙂	〰️	💣
Cat	💣	💣	🙂	🙂	🙂	🙂	💣	💣
Bird	💣	〰️	〰️	〰️	🙂	🙂	🙂❤️	〰️
Mice	💣	💣	💣	💣	🙂	💣	〰️	🙂

❤️ *Get along best*   💣 *Fur will fly*   〰️ *Indifferent to each other*   🙂 *Can learn to get along*

4 No Worries

By now, your rats have grown accustomed to your voice, your odor, and your hand. When a rat will crawl onto your hand willingly, gently stroke it between its ears or down its back. Tame rats are extremely fond of such petting. This is a great way to make friends with the furry little newcomer.

5 How to Pick Up a Rat

A rat's tail is not a handle. If you pick a rat up by its tail, the tail may break, or the skin may separate from the bones and pull right off. Instead, grasp the rat gently around its middle, supporting its legs with the other hand. You can hold your pet in two hands, or rest it in the crook of one arm.

6 Fast Friends

When your rat grooms itself as it sits on your shoulder or falls asleep tucked in your elbow, you know that you have passed the test of trust. The rats living together in a colony reinforce their bonds by grooming each other. If your pet licks you with its supple little tongue, take it as a compliment and a gesture of friendship.

1 **No obstacle**
Scrambling over a paper towel roll is fun—but it will be even more fun to shred the last few paper towels.

2 **Grooming**
Though roaming free offers enticing opportunities for adventure, Zippy doesn't neglect his grooming.

3 **In the picnic basket**
Flip can rummage around and explore to his heart's content, but he still feels sheltered inside the basket.

4 **Snack**
Zippy loves cucumber slices. This juicy tidbit will fortify him for more adventures.

HAVE FUN

Fun and Games with Rats

Rats have a strong need for activity and stimulation. They can't stand to be bored. In fact, these intelligent rodents will even invent games to amuse themselves. This lively group is having a grand time with a wooden block of "Swiss cheese."

Out of Sight, Out of Mind

Zippy and Flip have grown accustomed to my many visitors. At first, they were rather shy, preferring to stay in their cage until the guests had left. Now, however, they seem to enjoy the diversion; indeed, they often want to be right in the middle of the action. A few days ago, my friend Susan dropped by to return a book. Inviting her to stay a while, I set a bowl of potato chips on my wicker coffee table. As we chatted, Flip and Zippy scampered across the floor. In a flash, they climbed the table leg, clearly intending to help themselves to a little snack. When I firmly plopped them down on the floor again, they started such a rowdy scuffle that Susan and I couldn't help laughing. Finally, tuckered out, the little fellows made their way onto the couch and into their favorite hideaway—the sleeves of my sweater. Soon, all was quiet; they had fallen asleep. Susan and I returned to our conversation, and I forgot all about my two sleepyheads.

When Susan stood up to leave, I stood too and gave her a quick hug. Immediately, we heard startled squeaks of protest from my sweater sleeves. When I hugged Susan, I must have squeezed Flip and Zippy too! Chagrined, I drew them gently out and offered each little rat an extra morsel of fruit to make amends.

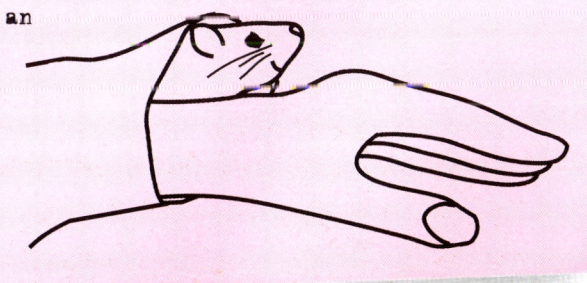

5. Hitch-hiker
Flip enjoys touring the house in a cozy jacket pocket.

6. Market basket
A climbing challenge and a tempting snack combined! Zippy has his eye on the radishes.

Common Hazards

➔ Be careful not to step on—or sit down on—your little pal.

➔ Rats creep and climb freely; don't accidentally shut them into a cupboard or drawer.

➔ If possible, secure electrical cords behind protective strips. Rats establish preferred paths; keep these free of cords.

➔ Close off any holes a rat might fall into.

➔ Be on guard about containers of water a rat could crawl into but not escape from (such as a vase or aquarium).

➔ Rats like to disappear under the sofa cushions, and they can also get into the innersprings.

➔ Keep doors and windows closed while your rats are roaming free.

HAVE FUN 41

have fun

3 Tumble ball
Also from the pet store, this hollow ball is great fun for a nimble explorer.

4 Wobbly blocks
Stir chopped fruit or kernels of grain into gelatin dessert mix and let it set in ice-cube trays. Your rats will relish this tasty snack.

HAVE FUN

Build an Adventure Playground

Offer your rats an ever-changing variety of opportunities to explore, climb, and play.

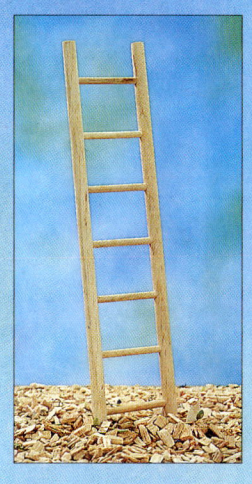

1 Ladder
Pet stores sell wooden ladders like this one. Place it where a rat can safely climb, swing, and balance.

2 Mini-Gym in the Cage
A teeter-totter with a little bell to ring, a sandbox to dig in, and a hanging fort of woven straw provide entertainment and exercise when your rats must stay in the cage.

HAVE FUN

An Adventure Playground for Rats

Left to their own devices, your rats will romp and explore underneath the sofa and behind the bookcase, where you can't see them. It's more fun for you—and better for your furniture—if you set up an adventure playground for your furry friends. Be sure to change the equipment often, so they won't get bored. You can even rotate the toys, bringing back an old favorite after storing it for a while. Exercise your own imagination and creativity in choosing components, but remember the basic principles: Everything must be safe, stable, and either disposable or easy to keep clean. If your rats haven't played with toys from the time they were small, you'll need to be patient until they overcome their natural caution and accept the playground.

Any new toy can be made more interesting with food. In fact, it's always a good idea to make your pets work a little for their treats. The challenge will stimulate their brains and exercise their muscles.

With this simple obstacle, a rat can scramble over the top or scoot through the hole.

HAVE FUN 47

What Is Your Rat's Personality Type?

Rats can have very different personalities. There are sensitive cuddly rats, confident fighters, indefatigable explorers, and active adventurers. Use this little test to determine which category describes your rat. Of course, a rat can fit in more than one category.

		YES	NO
1	When allowed to roam outside the cage, is your rat constantly on the move?	○	○
2	Does your rat prefer to spend its time on your lap or shoulder?	○	○
3	Does your rat view bookshelves not as an insurmountable obstacle, but as a challenge?	○	○
4	Does your rat enjoy tussling with your hand?	○	○
5	Will your rat sit still and let you stroke it for a long time while you do something else, such as talk on the phone?	○	○
6	Can your rat work away at cleverly packaged food until it solves the brain-teaser?	○	○
7	Does your rat prefer to avoid a scuffle when possible?	○	○
8	Does your rat tend to groom its comrades roughly, sometimes even pushing them down?	○	○
9	Do the other rats take a treat away from this one now and then?	○	○
10	Do you need to reinforce a simple cage door to keep your rat from figuring out how to open it?	○	○

Key: If you answered "yes" to questions 1, 3, and 4, your rat is an active adventurer; to 2 and 5, a cuddler. "yes" to questions 4 and 8 indicates a self-confident rat, dominant in the pack; "yes" to 7 and 9 suggests a submissive tendency. "yes" to questions 6 and 10 describes the tireless explorer.

8 **Tree root**

What fun to climb on and sniff at a sturdy tree root! It makes a great hiding place, too.

5 Cardboard box
How many ways can a rat find to crawl in and out of this homemade hideaway?

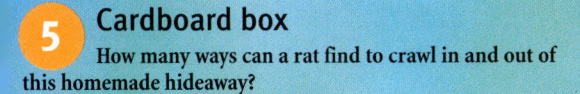

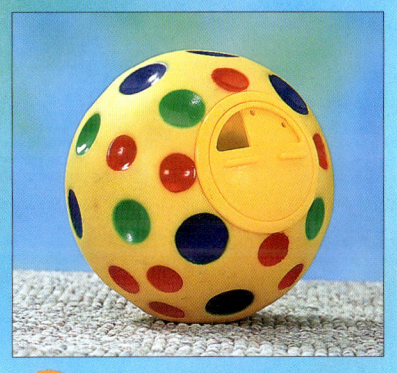

7 Snack dispenser
Fill a plastic ball like this one with tidbits of dry food. When the rat rolls the ball along the floor, the yummy morsels drop out one by one.

6 Little house and pine cone
Rats like to creep into an enclosed space where they can eat in peace. For a special treat, tuck nuts, raisins, or other dried fruit securely between the scales of a pine cone. Your rats will pluck them out with deft forepaws.

Play and Exploration

In the wild, rats use all their senses—smell, hearing, taste, touch, and sight—every day. They must find food, be on the watch for predators, maintain their social contacts in the colony, and make all sorts of decisions in an environment that changes constantly. A pet rat needs a similar level of stimulation. Time spent outside the cage adds variety to a pet rat's daily routine, and interaction with others of their species, as well as with humans, provides the necessary social contact. With a little imagination, you can entertain your rats in ways that are appropriate to their natural behavior and responses.

What Your Rats Like

Try these activities. Remember that you can always modify them to suit your own pet rats.

➔ Lay a trail of an intriguing scent that leads to a reward. A very little bit goes a long way. (Caution: The oil of coniferous trees is poisonous to rats.)

➔ Build an obstacle course out of pillows on the sofa.

➔ Use wooden blocks, cardboard boxes, and tubes to construct a maze of tunnels, like a wild rat's burrow.

➔ See if your rats like to play energetic games with you—wrestling, tag, hide-and-seek. Your hand is just the right size to be a good opponent, but take care to be gentle and nonthreatening.

➔ Anything that rustles will catch a rat's attention. Try rustling a piece of paper to attract your furry friends when it's time to return them to the cage after a period of free play.

➔ While you enjoy playing with your pets, take the time to

Most pet rats will treat a familiar human as an entertaining playmate.

HAVE FUN

How Happy Is Your Rat?

How much time do your rats spend outside the cage each day?	○ None *0 points*	○ 1 hour *1 point*	○ More *3 points*
Do your rats groom each other?	○ Never *0 points*	○ Sometimes *1 point*	○ Often *3 points*
Is the rat's fur smooth and shining?	○ Yes *3 points*	○ No *0 points*	
Has your rat lost weight?	○ Yes *0 points*	○ No *3 points*	
Does your rat like to lick at your hand now and then?	○ Yes *3 points*	○ No *0 points*	
Is your rat active and curious?	○ Yes *3 points*	○ Sometimes *1 point*	● Often *2 points*
Do your rats fight with each other?	○ Rarely *1 point*	○ Never *3 points*	○ Quite a lot *0 points*
Does your pet spend a great deal of time sleeping?	○ Yes *0 points*	○ No *3 points*	
How does your rat respond to new things, such as twigs to gnaw on?	○ Avoids them *0 points*	○ Sniffs at them *1 point*	○ Nibbles at them *3 points*
How would you describe the areas around your pet's mouth, nose, eyes, and anus?	○ Skin reddish, moist *0 points*	○ Clean and dry *3 points*	○ Hair a little matted *1 point*
What do your rat's eyes look like?	○ Dull *0 points*	○ Goopy *1 point*	○ Clear and bright *3 points*

0–10 points: This rat has problems. 10–18 points: Could be better. 18–25 points: Good, but not great. 25–33 points: The rat is in tip-top shape.

Soap Addiction

Flip has developed quite a fondness for the soap in my bathroom. He'll perform the most amazing climbing stunts, all for the sake of nibbling at that bar of soap. The other day, I realized that I hadn't seen the little fellow for a while—and also that I had forgotten to close the bathroom door. Sure enough, it didn't take me long to find him, just making his way up the towel that hung from a hook by the sink. A cautious step brought him onto the narrow edge of the sink itself. On the other side, in the soap dish, was the prize he sought. Was he bold enough to tiptoe around the sink, risking a fall? The alternative was to go down into the basin and up the other side—but the water faucet was dripping, and Flip is no fan of shower baths. I held my breath as he balanced on his slippery perch. Finally, he made up his mind. Down into the sink he plunged, ignoring the cold drops of water that splashed on his back. Up the other side he scrambled, slipping and sliding. At last, he reached the soap dish. After all that effort, I didn't have the heart to pick him up right away, so I gave him a few minutes to enjoy his soapy reward. Then I took him back where he belonged—and this time, I didn't forget to close the bathroom door behind me.

observe their behavior and their body language (ears, posture, fur, tail). What do they look like when they're scuffling with each other, or when all is peaceful? When they're wary and cautious? When they're relaxed? What are their favorite places and pathways? Which one is the boss?

Can Rats Learn Tricks?

Yes, rats can learn tricks, given patience and positive reinforcement. You must reward them when they do something right. Because rats don't understand punishment, you won't be able to break them of any bad habits (like digging at your houseplants or gnawing on electric cords). The only solution is to be extra watchful.

Biting

Tame rats bite very rarely, and only in extreme situations—when they are annoyed, afraid, or hurt. Misunderstandings may arise if you insert food between the bars of the cage, or if your hand smells strongly of food or lotion. Then the rat can't tell where the food stops and the person starts. If your rat takes your finger or hand tentatively between its teeth, it may be testing something it thinks might be edible. However, your pet may also be issuing a warning— "Stop it!"—that should be taken seriously, even if it doesn't hurt.

TIP from the PET STORE

Pet stores sell an endless variety of toys for parrots, dogs, and cats. Many of these will also stimulate and amuse your pet rats. Do be careful not to choose items of a size and shape that a rat might get stuck inside.

Clay pipes make a great place to sleep, but they're even more fun to explore.

OLD & HAPPY

Active and Happy

Bruno is two years old—a senior citizen among rats. When he was younger, every day was a big adventure. But now, he likes nothing better than a warm cozy place to snooze and plenty of quiet stroking. He's content to leave the adventures to the young ones.

in Old Age

OLD & HAPPY 53

old & happy

How Long Do Rats Live?

Pet rats live for only two to three years. Although the literature mentions rats that live longer than this, such exceptions are rare. In their natural living conditions, rats often survive for no more than six months to a year.

This short life span has disadvantages, but also advantages. On the one hand, it means that you must say good-bye only too soon to a familiar companion that has become a part of your life. On the other hand, when you choose to keep pet rats, your responsibility lasts for a relatively short time. By contrast, a dog may live for ten to fifteen years, and parrots live as long as thirty to 100 years.

How to Recognize an Older Rat

When your pet rat is about one and a half to two years old, you will begin to notice that its coat is a little coarser and its typically long face looks leaner and more angular. It loses interest in activity and explora-

The Autumn of Life

→ **Behavior:**
With age, rats grow calmer and less interested in adventure. Many a little dynamo now mellows into a snuggly companion.

→ **Appearance:**
A healthy rat has a smooth coat even in old age, though the fur may thin somewhat. A shaggy coat can be a sign of illness. The rat's long face looks increasingly lean and angular.

→ **Group Status:**
As once-dominant rats grow older and younger rats reach maturity, their relative rank in the pack changes.

→ **Diet:**
A healthy diet, with plenty of fruit and vegetables, is especially important at this stage of life. Be sure to limit an older rat's fat and protein intake.

→ **Senses:**
We don't know for certain whether a rat's vision, hearing, and sense of smell decline in old age.

→ **Health:**
Rats suffer a wide range of age-related problems, such as kidney and heart disease, respiratory ailments, and paralysis. However, tumors are by far the most common cause of death.

tion; often, an older rat tends to seek more human contact. Be mindful of its needs. Provide a warm and comfortable environment, with easy access to food, water, and sleeping place. Remember that elderly rats can't climb and jump as they once could.

Proper nutrition becomes especially important for your older rat. Be sure its diet is low in fat, salt, and protein. Offer plenty of fresh fruits and vegetables.

Now more than ever, take the time to pet and stroke your furry friend. With gentle fingers, be alert for the warning signs of health problems. Illnesses develop rapidly in small animals like rats, and early identification can make a difference.

Age-Related Diseases

Just like humans, rats suffer from a range of age-related illnesses. But even in such small creatures, many illnesses can be treated or at least the symptoms alleviated. For this reason, it's a good idea to take a sick rat to a veterinarian who specializes in small animals. Age-related diseases in rats include

→ Kidney problems, which mean a greater need for fluids (and also more urine output).

Even an old rat can learn new tricks. Tempted by a tasty morsel, Keena scoots through this little grass hoop.

TIP from the VETERINARIAN

Be sure that your older rat continues to drink plenty of water. You might want to add a few drops of fruit juice to enhance the taste. Older rats often suffer kidney problems, and adequate fluid intake is particularly important in such cases.

→ Heart problems, with symptoms including weakness, respiratory problems, loss of appetite, bloating, and a blue tip of the tail.
→ Paralysis, which unfortunately cannot be cured.
→ Skin diseases, because the weaker immune system offers less protection.
→ More frequent respiratory infections, for the same reason.
→ Tumors, the most common cause of death in rats.

In particular, rat owners should have a basic understanding of respiratory disorders and tumors in rats. Almost all rats suffer from mycoplasmosis, a chronic respiratory ailment that is not contagious to humans. Although so far there is no cure for the disease itself, secondary illnesses respond very well to antibiotics. The symptoms of respiratory illness are gasping for breath, constant sneezing and nasal discharge, and in severe cases, lethargy and loss of appetite. When a rat's respiratory passages are irritated, red droplets appear around its nose and eyes and in its nest material. This is not blood, but a red pigment (porphyrin) in the tear fluid.

If any of your rats have this ailment, you can make their lives much more comfortable by keeping the cage meticulously clean, because soiled bedding is very irritating to the respiratory passages.

Rat hobbyists continue to dispute whether the rat's susceptibility to tumors is the result of breeding or simply a normal trait. On the one hand, certain strains of laboratory rats are in fact used for cancer research because they have a tendency to develop tumors. On the other hand, laboratory rats and pet rats live much longer than wild rats, and therefore they might be expected to have a higher incidence of cancer, just as older humans do.

We do know that cancer is one of the most common causes of death in rats. Tumors are especially frequent in females. Although surgical removal of tumors is possible, it should be considered only if the rat still has a long life expectancy. Otherwise, surgery merely causes unnecessary stress.

How Rats Die

It's very sad to think of a pet suffering illness and death. And yet, perhaps it's a good idea to consider what you will do when a rat in your care falls seriously ill.

Animals experience pain and helplessness in the immediacy of the present moment, without any hope for improvement or thought of possible remedies. In the wild, a mortally ill animal has no chance of survival, and death does not linger.

One of the responsibilities of owning an animal is to protect it from suffering. If your rat can barely move, gasps for breath, stops grooming itself, doesn't eat, and seems to be in pain, you should take it to the veterinarian, who can put it out of its misery. Your familiar voice, touch, and odor will ease the way as your little pet falls asleep for the last time.

Saying Good-bye

Our tame rats are as affectionate as dogs, and each has a distinct personality. No wonder we miss them when they die. Some people think it's silly to mourn for a small animal. It's quite likely that they never had a pet themselves. There's no reason to be ashamed of shedding a few tears for your departed pet.

The death of a pet may well be a child's first encounter with the fundamental issues of death and grief, as well as a parent's first chance to model and teach an appropriate response. Of course, the veterinarian can dispose of a dead animal's remains, but you could also choose to bury the body in your own yard or garden. Especially for children, this offers a meaningful opportunity to express and acknowledge their sadness. After all, they have known this little creature for its whole life, played with it, cared for it, and grown fond of it. The ceremony of

This older rat knows that exercise is still important—and climbing is still fun.

burying the body and honoring the memory of their faithful friend makes it much easier to return to happier memories later.

When a Rat Loses Its Companion

Scientists ordinarily resist attributing emotions to animals. And yet, for social creatures such as rats, it's not too farfetched to speak of loss and loneliness. Rats definitely notice when a comrade disappears; they search for the missing rat, and they may grow lethargic or stop eating. Give them extra attention to distract them.

If you intend to continue keeping rats, you should add another rat soon. For guidance on how to introduce a new rat into an existing group, see page 35.

Keep in mind, however, that if you introduce a very young rat as a companion to a single older rat, you will most likely face the same problem again very soon. It might be preferable to let the old one continue to live alone, with plenty of extra stimulation.

In any case, you should never place very young rats with older males. They may not accept the younger newcomers.

Thorough grooming is essential even when a rat grows old. Expect to see your older rats take plenty of time with their daily health-and-beauty routine.

A Wild Ride

Bold little Zippy had a wild adventure yesterday. I was tidying my desk, clearing out odds and ends, as Zippy and Flip explored nearby. Dumping my collection of paper clips into a smaller jar, I set the larger jar on the floor and began to sort pens and pencils. Out of the corner of my eye, I could see Zippy investigating the empty jar. Soon he had turned it on its side, and before long he had crept right in, sniffing curiously. All at once, the jar began to roll. Zippy tried to back out, but his movement only made the jar roll faster. I watched in dismay, unable to move, as Zippy and the jar tumbled across the carpet. Luckily, the jar soon came to rest against the filing cabinet. With a pitiful squeak, Zippy wobbled out and staggered dizzily across the room to where I sat. I took the poor little thing in my hands and stroked his back, crooning gently. Of course, when Flip saw that Zippy was getting extra attention, he hustled right over for his share of cuddling. Only when all three of us had calmed down did I put my furry friends back on the floor and return to my chores.

Index

B
Babies	18–19
Bathing	11
Behaviors	23–24, 54
Biting	51
Bringing home	28–29
Burrow	16, 18, 23

C
Cage	7, 28–29
Cage materials	7
Cancer	56
Care	11
Castration	19
Caution	19, 21
Characteristics	16, 29, 48
Children	29–30, 57
Colony	14, 17–18
Colors	21–22
Companion	35, 58
Compatibility	35

D
Death	56–57
Digging	24
Diseases	55–56
Domestication	21–22

E
Equipment	7
Estrus	24

F
Feeding	9, 19, 33
Feeding dish	7
Females	18
Fighting	17
Food	9, 19, 54

G
Grains	9
Grooming	24, 34

H
Handling	34
Happiness	49
Hazards	38
Health	54–56
Hearing	23
Hiding	24
Hiding places	7
History	14

I
Instincts	36

L
Life span	54

M
Males	18

N
Nest building	23

O
Odors	23, 30, 32–33
Offspring	18–19
Older rat	54–55

P
Pair of rats	35
Personality type	47
Picking up	34
Play	48
Playground	42–46

Q
Quiz	25

R
Roaming	36–38

S
Senses	22–23, 54
Sexual maturity	21
Shavings	11
Smell	23

INDEX

Tameness	28
Taste	23
Teats	19
Teeth	24, 30
Territory:	
marking of	23
protection of	16–17
Touch	23
Toys	11, 39, 43–46, 51
Tree root	46
Tricks	51
Trimming claws	11
Trust	28, 32–34
Tumble ball	44

Vacation	64–65
Veterinarian	65
Vision	22–23

Water	9

Monika Lange
studied biology with a major in zoology. A freelance journalist and the author of children's books and pet care handbooks, she has lived in Seattle, Washington since 1998. Among her other activities, she works as a volunteer at Woodland Park, one of the leading zoos in the United States.

Christine Steimer
is a dedicated animal photographer. She works for international book publishers, specialized journals, and advertising agencies.

Gabriele Linke-Grün
has worked for many years as a freelance writer for the Gräfe und Unzer nature book series and for various animal magazines and textbook publishers. She wrote our *Rat Adventures*.

A lively game of follow-the-leader is great fun.

ADDRESSES

Organizations

American Society of
  Mammologists
Monte L. Bean
Life Sciences Museum
Brigham Young University
Provo, UT 84602-0200
http://asm.wku.edu/

American Veterinary Medical
  Association
1931 N. Meacham Rd., Suite 100
Schaumburg, IL 60173-4360
www.avma.org

Rat Clubs

Rat Fan Club
857 Lindo Lane
Chico, CA 95973
(530) 899-0605
e-mail: ratlady@sunset.net

Rat & Mouse Club of America
13075 Springdale Street
  PMB 302
Westminster, CA 92683
www.rmca.org

American Fancy Rat and Mouse
  Association
9230 64th Street
Riverside, CA 92509-5924
www.afrma.org

Rat, Mouse, and Hamster
  Fanciers
Joyce Starkey, Secretary
2309 County Ranch Drive
Modesto, CA 95355
(209) 551-6332
e-mail: jstarkey@telis.org
www.ratmousehamster.com

Acknowledgments

The photographer and the publisher wish to thank the firm of Wagner & Keller of Ludwigshafen, Germany, for its gracious support. The company has worked successfully for many years to promote suitable conditions in bird and animal shelters.

Important Note

This guide tells the reader how to care for pet rats. The author and the publisher consider it important to alert the reader that the advice given in this book is intended primarily for normally developed rats specifically bred and raised to be pets and acquired from a reputable source. This means a rat breeder or pet dealer whose animals combine excellent breeding, good temperament, and vigorous health.

Anyone who acquires a pet rat from any other source should be aware that the animal has already formed its basic impressions of human beings as a result of the handling it has experienced. The owner should be sure to carefully observe all newly acquired rats, noting their reaction to humans and other animals in the home, making any allowances necessary. If possible, the new owner should try to learn the circumstances under which the rat had been maintained. It is also wise to have a qualified veterinarian examine the rat thoroughly when it is first acquired.

Rats may sometimes harbor diseases that are communicable to human beings. If your pet rat shows any symptoms of disease, consult your veterinarian immediately. If you have any questions about your own health or that of a family member, see your own doctor without delay.

English translation
© Copyright 2002 by
Barron's Educational Series, Inc.

Original title of the book
in German is
Meine Ratte und ich

Copyright © 2000 by Gräfe und
Unzer Verlag GmbH, Munich.

English translation by
Celia Bohannon

All rights reserved.

No part of this book may be reproduced in any form, by photostat, microfilm, xerography, or any other means, or incorporated into any information retrieval system, electronic or mechanical, without the written permission of the copyright owner.

*All inquiries should
be addressed to:*
Barron's Educational Series, Inc.
250 Wireless Boulevard
Hauppauge, NY 11788
http://www.barronseduc.com

*Library of Congress Catalog Card
No. 00-112033*

*International Standard Book
No. 0-7641-1922-2*

Printed in Hong Kong

9 8 7 6 5 4 3 2 1

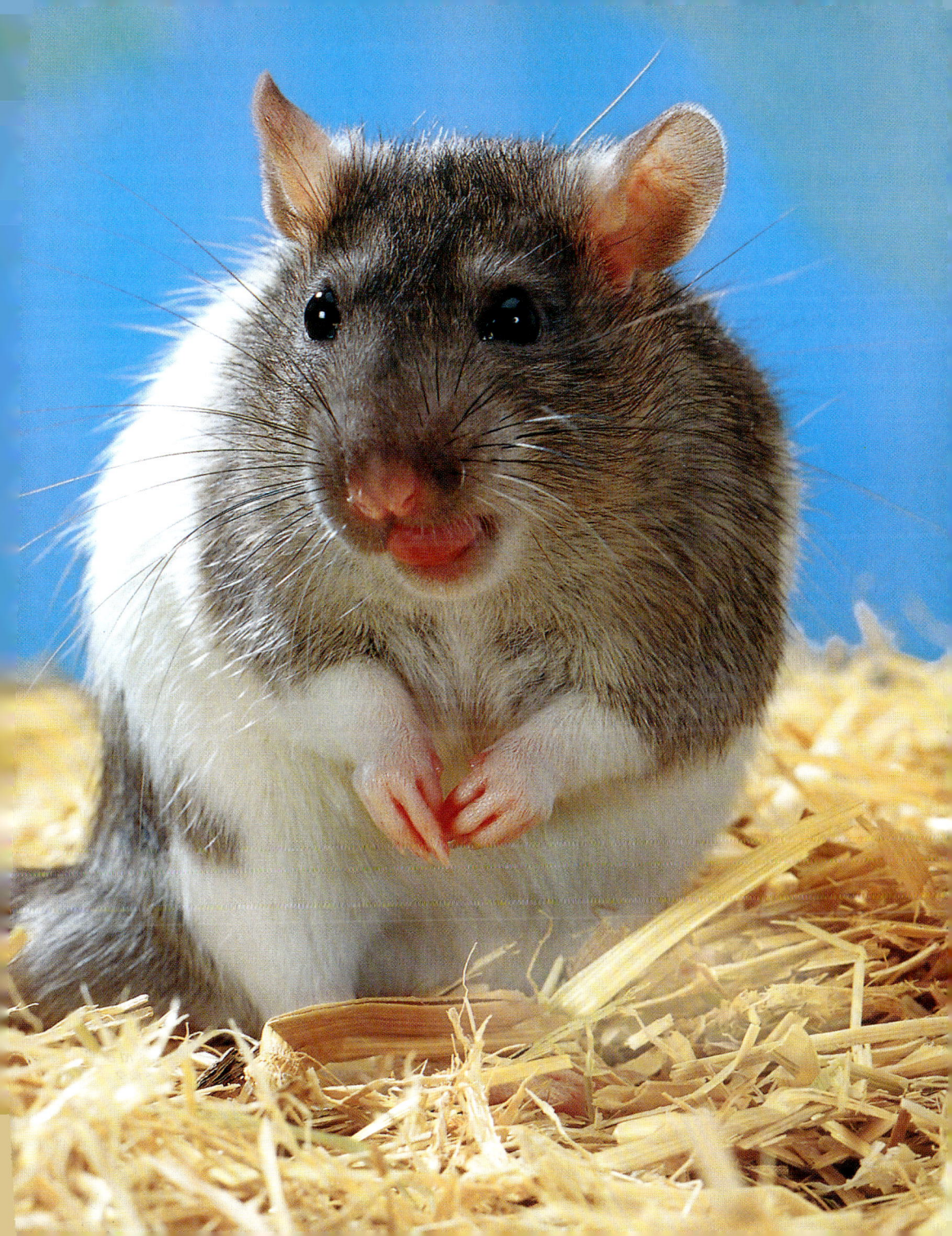

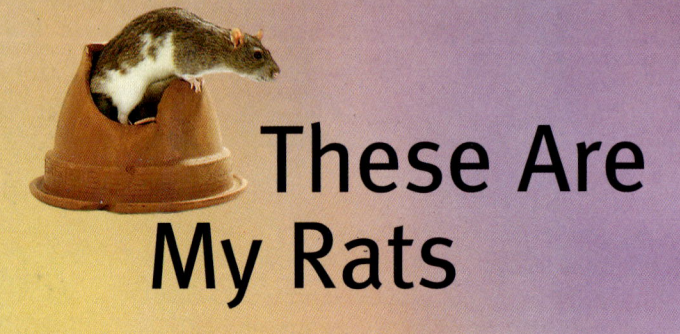

These Are My Rats

If you go away on vacation, or if you are sick, a friend or neighbor might have to take care of your pets for a while. In the spaces below, you can write helpful notes about your rats.

My rats' names:
1. ....
2. ....

What my rats look like:
1. ....
2. ....

How I recognize my rats:
1. ....
2. ....

Favorite special treats:
....
....

Tips for handling my rats:
....
....

How to take care of my rats:
....
....

Favorite activities:
....
....